MW01241725

Poems FROM

MY GOD
the road to life

BY CAROL BREEDEN

TATE PUBLISHING, LLC

DEDICATION

When **God** gives us a child, it is only appropriate that we dedicate that child back to Him. Likewise, I dedicate this book to **God**, because He gave it to me. I gave birth to it, but God is the true author. I thank Him for trusting me with the messages contained herein. I also dedicate this book to my late husband, **William (Rock) Breeden, Sr.** who encouraged me to seek God more diligently. **Rock**, I wish you were here to share this with me, but I know you are in a better place and would not want to return to earth.

ACKNOWLEDGMENTS

I would like to acknowledge three friends who were my biggest cheering section as I birthed each poem–**Claudia McAlister, Murel Chesser and Marina Valley**. Without them, I would not have had the courage to continue. They were the ones who convinced me that God was doing something special through me. Thank you, dear friends, for your faith in God and in me.

I would also like to thank my son and daughter, **Patrick Meeks** and **Colleen Murphy**, for their encouragement and support. Although they now have homes and children of their own, they still have time for their mother, and they still give me great joy.

I pray that my stepchildren, **William (Rock) Breeden, Jr.** And **Saundra Breeden** will be blessed by this book, because they should be able to see their father in some of the poems.

I acknowledge each of my grandchildren–**Cory, Caitlin, Colton, Grayson, Matthew, Kyle and Ryan.** You are an inspiration to me. I want to encourage each of you to submit your life to God and follow Him. Then you will never be disappointed with where life leads you, because you will be led by the Creator of life.

I thank **Bob and Murel Chesser** for assisting me in the editing process of this book.

FOREWORD

In Matthew's gospel Jesus declared, "Out of the overflow of the heart, the mouth speaks . . . For the good man brings good things out of the good stored up in him!" With pen in hand, and her heart in his hand, she writes. She brings forth the good stored up within herself, at any hour of the day, morning . . . noon . . . or night . . . as she writes. She ever stands poised to share her deepest thoughts and emotions with any and all who will dare to listen. Her poems are more than ritualistic rhymes; they are the earnest echo of her own struggles and victories of this thing we call life. You will be quick to identify with her heart stirrings and her inner cravings for God and God alone! My prayer is that you are blessed, as I have been, in listening in on the conversations between a lover of God and her precious Lord! God bless you as you begin this journey of divine intimacy.

Craig Dacus, Pastor
Bethesda Assembly of God Church
Oklahoma City, Oklahoma

INTRODUCTION

The writing of these poems has been a journey–the trek of a caterpillar being transformed into a butterfly. With each poem, there occurs a change within me. I gradually become aware of who I am, what I believe. There was a time in my life when I was easily persuaded, easily influenced by others around me. Not by everyone. Just certain people. Those who were stronger in character. Those who were good at manipulating. However, God used all that to form me into what He wants me to be.

I thought the death of my husband was the end of my life. It was just the beginning. For months I thought it vital to replace him, to fill that void. I now know that is not the answer. I now have a feeling of completeness. Completeness in God. You see, God is! And He is the rewarder of those who diligently seek Him.

Through the steps of my husband's illness with cancer, his subsequent death, and then later my trying to make some sense out of life, I would cry out to God when I found myself floundering, sinking in despair. God was always there when I cried out to Him. He still is. It's as if He walks me through a very difficult time and then He helps me pour out my thoughts, my innermost being, on paper. I search inside of myself for the words to describe what I am feeling, and He gives me the words. That is why I entitled the book *Poems From My God.*

I say "my" God because He is very personal to me; we are intimate friends. I hope He is your God too, because He is so awesome. It hurts to think that there are people who do not know Him. Through my poems, I am sharing that intimate friendship with God. If you don't know Him, I pray that you will come to know Him. If you know Him just a little, I pray that you will come to know Him more intimately. If you already know Him intimately, I invite you to bask in His presence as I share with you just what He means to me and how He is forming me into what He meant me to be.

Carol Breeden
December 19, 2004

CONTENTS

LET ME INTRODUCE YOU

Let me introduce you
To someone who is my friend
He's the Alpha and Omega
The beginning and the end

Wonderful, Counselor
A mighty God is He
He is Jehovah Rophe
The one who healeth thee

Everlasting Father
The Prince of Peace is He
There's no one better you could know
When'er you have a need

He is a friend who will stick
Closer than a brother
If you should find you need a friend
Like Him there is no other

There are those who mock and jeer
At the mention of His name
But when they stand before Him
They'll drop their head in shame

For then they'll know without a doubt
The things they'd heard were true
He did come and walk on earth
And He died for me and you

July 1986

LOST IN THE STRUGGLE

Lost in the struggle of life and death
Wanting to die more than to live
Not understanding the powers at hand
Or the grace He did give

Swallowed up in darkness
So dreary and so glum
Wanting to find my way out
Oh, but from which way did I come?

Alas! A light I do see
In my heart it is raised
As I lift my soul to Thee
In adoration and praise

Yes, He shows me the way
He is ever so near
Ever patiently waiting
For my heart to hear

March 1987

IF YOU ONLY KNEW

If you only knew what I have in store for you

If you only knew what I have prepared for you

If you only knew that your place in eternity is far more important than your place in this world

If you only knew that it is more important to learn the lessons I am trying to teach you

If you only knew that the cares of this world are trivial compared to the things going on in the spiritual realm

If you only knew how much I could do in your life if you would only let go and walk in My ways

If you only knew, you would do things so much differently

If you only knew!

(Lord, please help us to REALLY know!)

August 29, 2001

LETTER FROM JESUS

You are My child, and I am well pleased with you. I ask that you keep your spirit open to Me. Communicate with Me every day. Come to Me when you are happy and when you are sad. Turn to Me when you are hurting inside. People in the world will hurt you, just like they did Me. They crucified Me, but that was all in the Father's plan. I went to the Cross so that you could be free, so that you could have peace, so that you could have forgiveness and in turn, forgive those around you who trespass against you. Do not be angry or bitter when others trespass against you. Instead, turn to Me and ask for My help. I will always be there. I will never leave you nor forsake you. You cannot always count on the people around you to be there for you when you need them, but *I WILL ALWAYS BE THERE.* I AM everywhere at all times. I see everything. I hear everything. I know everything. Nothing escapes Me. I know your thoughts. I know your fears. I know your sorrows. I also know there is love in your heart–love for Me. I want to put *more* love in your heart. I want to direct your paths. I want to give you the life that My Father planned for you. *SEEK ME.* Turn to Me for all your needs, wants and desires. Put your life in My hands, and I will make something beautiful of your life. I love you.

JESUS

July 12, 2002

CONVERSATION WITH THE LORD

Why am I here
What would You have me to do
Pray to the Father, through the Son
Pray that the battle will be won

But isn't that a given, Lord
Regardless of what I do
I don't understand Thee
Lord, why do You need me

It's not so much that I need you
As it is that you need Me
I can do this on My own
But then, where would you be

On the outside looking in
As a stranger, not a friend
But Lord, why do I have a part
Because I am in your heart

I am a part of you and
You are a part of Me
We are to work together
For all the world to see

But sometimes I feel so helpless
I don't know what to do
That is the time to yield to Me
And let Me work through you

Lord, though I tell them about You
It seems my words do not get through
Do I continue again and again
Though it seems to be in vain

So it seemed when I was there
Was there anyone to really care
In sin and sorrow, pain and strife
They continued on with their own life

But I came for one purpose
That was to bridge the way
For those who would, to come
Never again to stray

You may never see
This side of eternity
If the things you say and do
Ever really get through

But if your mind is stayed on Me
And your words are those I give
Then that is why you're here
That is why you live

Lift up My name
I'll draw all men to Me
Your work won't be in vain
Soon all the world will see

I AM the Christ
I AM the Risen One
I AM the true Messiah
I AM God's only Son

So do not cease to speak of Me
Your words won't be in vain
Let every thought and every deed
Be done in Jesus' name

April 2003

COME HOME

My child, do not grieve
For, lo, I am with you
My rod and My staff
They shall comfort you

For such a time as this
You have been prepared
For such a time as this
Your heartache will be shared

Your victory lies in Me
That all the world should see
Your hope is not deferred
For all your prayers I've heard

Turn your face toward Me
Seek Me every day
My strength will flow to thee
As you seek My face and pray

Pray as you've never prayed before
Immerse yourself in My Word
Then you shall claim victory
Then you shall be heard

When My people humble themselves
And seek My face and pray
That is when they'll hear from Me
Every night and every day

The life I give to you is sacred
You must guard it carefully
Do not waste a single moment
Do not treat it carelessly

I have given you but one life on earth
And then your days shall end
So seek Me, seek the new birth
That is when your life will truly begin

You cannot have this world
And have true life with Me
You must choose one or the other
You must choose your destiny

Let go of your life
And reach out to Me
For when you let go
That's when you shall see

You will know who I truly am
You will know just why I came
You will trust your life to Me
And you will never be the same

Your life will be a holy one
Untouched by sin and shame
You will walk a different pathway
And I will give you a new name

So let go
Let Me have My way
Do not be afraid
For this is what you'll say

I let go and walked to Him
And that is when my life began
No more darkness, no more fear
He is ever present, ever near

A love I could not fathom
So peaceful and so pure
I could not comprehend
I could not ask for more

In Him I am made complete
In Him I am fulfilled
He is everything I've longed for
Heaven on earth in me instilled

So come
Come one, come all
Come unto Me
Come and heed My call

Bow to Me
And Me alone
Come, My beloved
Come home

June 8, 2003

YOUR REDEMPTION DRAWETH NIGH

My child, I told you
That I would be there
I told you
I would answer your prayer

When you humbled yourself
And sought My face
When you turned to Me
And sought My grace

For it is grace
And grace alone
For it is grace
That will see you home

The works that I did
While on earth
Healing, teaching
And giving new birth

Have all been handed
On to you
To bring new life
And power anew

This is not the time
To lay back and rest
This is the time
To give Me your best

Your best is everything
You have to give
Your time, your thoughts
The way you live

22

Give your all
And nothing less
For what you give
Is what I bless

It's up to you
And you alone
Whether you retreat
Or come home

To come home
Is to turn to Me
Seek My face
Seek all of Me

Yield to Me in every way
Relax in Me every day
Enter My rest and you will see
Enter My rest and you will be

All things at all times
To those around
For they will sense in you
What they have not found

They will feel your strength
Your peace and your love
They will know it could only
Come from above

They will reach out to you
To show them the way
They will willingly come
They will willingly pray

Pray as they've never
Prayed before
They will taste Me
And they will want more

Lift up My name
I will draw all men to Me
Lift up My name
And all the world will see

The Holy One
The One who came
God's only Son
Who will rule and reign

They will reach out to Me
And they will receive
Life everlasting
When they believe

For the time is here
But have no fear
The hour has come
All will be won

Lift up your eyes
Unto the skies
Your redemption
Draweth nigh

June 14, 2003

HIS HEART'S CRY

Lift up your eyes unto the skies
For your redemption draweth nigh
I will never leave you nor forsake you
I will always be nearby

Put your trust in Me
Praise Me every day
Then all your fears will vanish
And I'll wipe your tears away

Give Me all your praise
For you can never praise Me enough
Give Me all your love
For you can never love Me too much

Every hour of every day
I seek for thee
Oh, how My Spirit longs
To draw you close to Me

Sometimes you come so close
And then you move away
I long so much for you to come
Close to Me and stay

I grieve for you when you're hurting
I long for you when you're lonely
Oh, if you only knew
Oh, if only

I search for you at night
I look for you during the day
You were with me just briefly
And then you went away

25

Why do you go
When I want you to stay
I want you close by
Every night and every day

How can I take care of you
When you won't stay by My side
And when I come in search of you
You run away and hide

Yet you cry out to Me
And wonder where I am
Don't you know I'm right here
Waiting for you to let Me in

I must have all of you
You can hold nothing back
And when you give your all to Me
There will be nothing you will lack

For you, I came to earth
For you, I gave My life
For you, I bled and died
Twas the ultimate sacrifice

Was it all for naught
Was it all in vain
For you reject Me
And you stay the same

Come, I beseech you
Come unto Me
Come and let Me change you
Into what I meant for you to be

June 29, 2003

SHOW ME THE WAY HOME

Lord, I come to You
And to You alone
I heed Your call
To come home

Show me how
To abide in You
Teach me, Lord
What I should do

I come now
And sit at Your feet
I pray this will be
A time we will meet

I need to know
That You are here
I need to know
That You care

Let me hear Your voice
Let me feel Your touch
I need You, Lord
Oh, I need You so much

Show me the way
That I should go
Teach me the things
I need to know

For You are the potter
And I am the clay
Mold me and make me
Yours today

Change me into what
You meant me to be
Don't leave me here
In my iniquity

Without You I am nothing
And, oh, so alone
Come take my hand
And lead me home

I want to stay
Close by Your side
I do not want
To run and hide

I want to give
My all to You
Please, Lord, show me
What to do

Take my hand
And lead the way
Walk with me
Every day

I need for You
To lead the way
And keep me, Lord
I humbly pray

For it's You I want
And You alone
Please, dear Lord
Show me the way home

August 25, 2003

THE CHOICE

Up to now
You've tasted drops of Me
But I want to send to you
Blessings as from the sea

A body of water
So tumultuous and deep
That when you immerse yourself
You will cry out to Me and weep

Tears of joy
And tears of sorrow
Tears of yesterday
Today and tomorrow

Old things will pass away
A time of cleansing will take place
I will make you a new creature
I'll put a shine upon your face

For you are Mine, you know
Your old life is no more
In you, I'm starting a new thing
And placing you on a distant shore

On that distant shore
You will see
More than you've ever seen before
Far into eternity

The things that seem so far away
Will now be close to you
And the things that were so close
Will be gone, forever and a day

As you meditate on My Word
As you spend time in My presence
I will share things with you
I will show you My very essence

There are many things
I want to tell you
There are many things
You need to know

But you have to sit
Patiently by My side
And you must resist that urge
To run away and hide

For I've given you the freedom
To come to Me, or go
I pray you'll choose to come
For there's so much you need to know

Secrets of the universe
I want to share with you
And if you will just come
I'll show you what to do

The time is so short
There's much we need to do
So come sit with Me a while
I'll share these things with you

You want to know just what to do
You want to know just what to say
Spend some time with Me
Then I'll send you on your way

You'll know what to do
You'll know what to say
But you'll have to return
To Me every day

For I am your lifeline
Your light and your source
Draw from Me what you need each day
Then I'll pour you out on the world once more

Tis a life like no other
You can heed it, or turn away
The choice is up to you
You can go, or you can stay

If you stay, it will be
All of you, for all of Me
The decision is yours
What will it be?

September 22, 2003

A VESSEL

I am Thine, O Lord
And I seek to do Thy will
Here I am, I yield to You
Here's my cup, please fill

As I walk on earth today
Let me be aware of those in need
May Your Spirit be strong in me
So Your every prompting I'll heed

There's so many out there hurting
There's so many who are lost
I want to reach out and help them
And never count the cost

Will I be able to do this
Can I yield myself to You
Oh, I pray that I'll be worthy
Knowing my worth comes from You

Draw me ever closer to You
And fill me with Your love
Make me what You meant me to be
Send Your power from above

Make me, mold me, fill me, use me
O Lord, that is my plea
A gold or silver vessel
Dear Lord, please make of me

I look at myself closely
I do not like what I see
There are so many reasons why
A vessel I cannot be

But You said if I would come
And yield myself to Thee
You would make me a new creature
And You would put Your Spirit in me

So come and do Your work in me
Leave no stone unturned
Shine Your light on every darkness
Let all sin be burned

A clean and shining vessel
Is what I want to be
So that You can use me
So through Your eyes I'll see

When I look at others
Let me see what You see
Not their faults and failings
But what You know they can be

If I can make one heart a little lighter
In one life bring a little peace
Help a lost one along the way
And where there's bondage, bring release

Then my life will have meaning
It won't all be in vain
For this is why You took human form
This is why You came

So Your work will continue
As it was meant to be
So lives will be changed
And spiritual eyes will see

November 22, 2003

JESUS

I belong to Jesus
I am His and He is mine
He will be with me forever
And forever I am Thine

His presence is so beautiful
The peace, the joy, the love
I bask in the tranquility
That comes only from above

The peace that passeth
All of my understanding
Calms my fear and trembling
Never, ever demanding

The joy of the Lord
Is my strength and my portion
It keeps my heart singing
Full of joy and exhortation

The love that I experience
Like nothing ever felt before
So pure and so radiant
Glorious, and so much more

My God is an awesome God
Like Him there is no other
To me He is so wonderful
My Father, my Friend, my Brother

Have you ever met Him
Do you call Him by name
Do you know what He did for you
Do you know why He came

He came so you might have life
And life more abundantly
That you'd not live in fear and strife
And that His love you'd see

He yearns for you to come
To take Him at His word
And in faith believe
The Good News that you've heard

He came to redeem you
To show you the way
He wants you to accept Him
He wants you to say

Jesus, I believe in You
In all You've said and done
I ask that You forgive me
Make me your daughter or son

Come into my heart
And my life please change
My cluttered up life
Please rearrange

Make me, mold me, form me
Into what You meant for me to be
Give me the assurance
Of Your presence for eternity

For when you have done this
You will never be the same
You will understand the mystery
You will know why He came

December 6, 2003

GONE HOME

I looked down upon his face
As I tucked him into bed
You're going to lose him, said my heart
But not a tear was shed

You see, a few days before
When a bad report was given
I said, Thy will be done, O Lord
You've the right to take him to Heaven

He's Yours, dear Lord, I said
I will accept whatever You do
Though I would like for him to stay
You may take him home with You

The journey that we were given
I do not wish on anyone
But I wouldn't trade it for anything
Even though now he's gone

Our last days were tender and peaceful
No more contention and strife
Many hugs throughout each day
We now looked differently on life

Not one step could be taken
Without Jesus by our side
In Him we put our trust
In Him we did abide

Though he didn't get to stay
In fact, he wanted to go
I do not feel forsaken
I am not filled with woe

His passing was so peaceful
A smile upon his face
His spirit left this earth
Completely filled with grace

He belongs to Jesus now
For in death we do part
But a special place he'll always have
Deep within my heart

Lord, You know what's best
You have Your plans for me
I look forward eagerly
To what lies ahead with Thee

December 13, 2003

GLORY

You are forgiven
You are the apple of My eye
I trust you
Do you want to know why?

Because you return My love
Your heart cries out to Me
You long to be in My presence
My face you yearn to see

You feel so undeserving
You wonder why I care
Without Me you'd be lost
You wouldn't have a prayer

I created you
And I love you
That is why
I take care of you

I died for you
Don't you see?
I loved you
Before you loved Me

I created you
For a purpose
You are to join Me
In My service

Service to those
Around you in need
Reach out and touch them
Scatter My seed

For you have hidden treasure
Deep inside of you
You are My vessel
Tried and true

The things you feel
Deep down inside
Come from Me
For with Me you abide

So do not be afraid
Of what you feel
Deep down inside you
It's Me, it's real

I will lead you
I will guide you
I will stay
Close beside you

Walk with Me
Talk with Me
Pour your heart
Out to Me

For then
You will see
IT IS REAL
It is ME

I AM inside of you
That's the whole story
Christ in you
The hope of Glory!

January 12, 2004

THE COMMISSION

My Church, come forth
Rise up and walk
In the ways of your Lord
Don't just talk the talk

I am commissioning you
To go forth to all the nations
Healing and delivering
And mending broken relations

Make the lame to walk
Give sight to the blind
Breathe in life to the dead
And deliver from evil of all kind

This is why you are here
This is why I gave you life
To be My loving ambassadors
To quench all contention and strife

I have put My Spirit in you
My Word is in your heart
You have been equipped
Each to do his part

Don't look to each other
Measuring yourself in their eyes
But look to Me for direction
I'll never be in disguise

You'll always know it's Me
For in your heart I'll speak
You'll know My very nature
When it's Me you seek

So turn the TV off
Computer games can wait
It's time to do My work
For the time is getting late

You must not be complacent
In your relationship with Me
For I am your only lifeline
Without Me you wouldn't be

Those earthly things you so desire
Count them all as dung
There are more important things at hand
The last round has begun

This is My final call
To those with ears to hear
To those whose hearts will listen
And to those who really care

Take up your shield and sword
Put on the Armor of God
Go forth with mighty fury
As through the earth you trod

This is My commission
My plans you all will see
Fulfilled before your very eyes
Oh, what a feat it will be

So spiritual ears, open and hear
Spiritual eyes, open and see
Go forth, in the name of the Lord
And claim the victory!

January 19, 2004

THE CALL

My children, come
Come to Me now
I long to hold you close
And kiss you on your brow

I've loved you since
The beginning of time
I've always loved you
For you are Mine

If you only knew
My plans for you
You wouldn't keep doing
The things that you do

You would run to Me
Into My embrace
You would hold Me tight
And kiss My face

For I AM your God
And I love you so
I'm holding on to you
And I won't let you go

I'm always right here
You'll never be alone
And one of these days
I'll take you home

To the place that I
Have prepared for you
But before that time
We've work to do

It's not for **you** to choose
The work that you will do
But you must yield to Me
and **I'll** show you what to do

You each have a part
In My plan to carry out
You must get into position
So we can be about

The plans of the Father
Through the Son
By the Holy Spirit
The Three in One

The work will be quick
You'll hardly bat an eye
And before you know it
You'll ascend to the sky

You'll hear My shout
We'll meet in the air
But right now
It's time to prepare

Let go of those things
That so easily beset you
And come to Me
I'll lead and guide you

SO RIGHT NOW, come to **ME**
And let Me mold you
Into that person
I meant for you to be!

January 20, 2004

MY FATHER

Oh, my Father
How I love You
How I worship
And adore You

For You are
My everything
My hope, my strength
The song I sing

In the darkness
You are my light
When I can't see
You are my sight

When I am lonely
My friend You are
When I need You
You're never far

You are so peaceful
Loving and pure
How can I tell You
How great You are

Words can't describe
The love that I feel
Knowing You're here
Knowing You're real

Knowing I'll never
Be without You
You're mine forever
A dream come true

Oh, how You shine
You light up my life
You block out all darkness
Contention and strife

Right here with You
I want to stay
Never to leave You
Never to go away

For Your presence
Is so awesome
And when I truly seek You
You always come

You bid me to come
Closer to You
Of course, I'll come
What else could I do

For here in Your presence
I want to stay
Communing with You
Every day

January 21, 2004

MY HEART'S CRY

Here I am, Lord
I stand before You now
I worship and adore You
And before You now I bow

My gift to You
Is all of me
I consecrate myself
Wholly to Thee

Take from my life
Whatever You please
I hold onto nothing
Other than Thee

Cleanse me completely
My Father, I pray
Form something beautiful
Out of this clay

For by myself I'm nothing
Never anything grand
Only if I'm formed
By the Master's hand

So form me
And fine tune me
Make me an instrument
Only for Thee

Keep my eyes on You
Never let me stray
For You know I want to be
Completely Yours from this day

Whisper to me
What You want me to do
Whatever it is
I'll do it for You

Pour Your Spirit
Into me
A triple portion
I ask of Thee

Then gently guide me
And whisper in my ear
My ear is open
Your voice I want to hear

Tell me Your secrets
The things I need to know
Give me direction
And that is where I'll go

I do not take this lightly
A whim it's not to me
My heart cries out completely
For Yours I want to be

January 27, 2004

TRUST

Dear Lord, Let my thoughts
Be Your thoughts

Let my words
Be Your words

You will bring forth
Your perfect creation
In Your own time

Yes, I must do my part
Which is to keep my eyes on You
And to give my all to You

My efforts will not change anything
But Your Spirit will change all things

I must let go of everything
I must trust You in everything

When You become the most
Important thing to me
Then all will be well with my soul

January 28, 2004

ADORATION

Lord, I thank You for who You are
I thank You for all that You do
There is absolutely no one
Who can compare to You

You are my salvation
You are my peace
When I turn to You in trouble
I always find release

You are the King of kings
You are the Lord of lords
You are my all in all
My everything and more

I bask in Your presence
You are so good to me
I never want to lose You
Your face I long to see

Lord, I am so glad
You bid me to come
I just want to tell You
My heart You have won

I know I can trust You
You've never let me down
I put all my hope in You
My faith in You is sound

I know my feet are
On solid ground
For a firm foundation
In You I have found

In You, I've put my trust
In You, I do rest
You said to try You, and I did
And yes, You passed the test

You are who You say You are
You do what You say You'll do
In You I have full assurance
For I find no fault in You

So I give my life to You
To do with as You please
With no hesitation
My heart is filled with ease

Your plans for me
I do not know
But they will be good
Because You love me so

Your love for me I have
Accepted as true
No one has ever loved me
As much as You

The things You've done for me
I will never, ever forget
No more will I worry
No more will I fret

Lord, I bow down to You
In worship and adoration
I thank You and give to You
All my love and admiration

January 31, 2004

LET GO AND LET GOD

Whenever you feel
Tension and strife
Know that they don't
Belong in your life

Turn to Jesus
Ask Him for His help
Know He will always
Show you a way out

He wants to help you
He wants to set you free
He wants to make you
What He meant you to be

But first you have to
Invite Him in
Yield to Him and
Repent from sin

He is always waiting
Listening for your cry
He'll never forsake you
And here's the reason why

He created you
You are His child
A masterpiece
He knew all the while

As He formed you
And planned your days
He knew what would happen
He knew all your ways

There is not another
One like you
You are unique
In everything you do

He watches over you
His Word to perform
Though trials He will bring
He'll cause you no harm

So count it all joy
When those trials come
And yield to Him
The Great and Mighty One

Tell Him how you feel
Cry out with all your heart
Ask Him to deliver you
Tell tension and strife to depart

It takes but a moment
To cry out to Him
Don't yield to temptation
Don't carry out sin

Temptations will come
About that there's no doubt
We all have to face them
But alone, we can't work them out

So when temptation comes
To strike back at others
Remember they are
Your sisters and brothers

We all are a part
Of God's family
For He grafted us into
His Family Tree

One another's burdens
We are to share
To help and encourage
To let them know we care

So do not hang on
To tension and strife
Give them to Jesus
So you may have life

Let go and let God
Have His way with you
He's always there
And He knows what to do

February 2, 2004

HUNK OF CLAY

I feel so battered
So black and blue
Why, oh why
I beg of You

Will life always
Hurt so much
I cry out to You
I need Your touch

I feel so very peaceful
And then it's snatched away
Yesterday was good
But then came today

Today was torture
Today was so bad
I lost all the peace
I thought I ever had

Where were You
Were You by my side
Did You feel my hurt
When I ran away and cried

What is happening to me
I don't know who I am
O God, it hurts so much
Is this part of Your plan?

If it is
Then that's okay
But, O God
I need You today

When I asked You for
A triple portion
Was that You
Or mere distortion

It seemed to me
From my spirit it came
I wanted more of You
Not just more of the same

But more of You
Brings more sorrow
At least for today
But what about tomorrow

What will tomorrow bring
Will I be able to stand
Or will I simply crumple
While on my face I land

You told me not
To run away and hide
But that's what I want to do
In You I do confide

Is this a part
Of Your stripping away
Of Your reshaping
This hunk of clay

If it is
Then please continue
I'll accept whatever
Is on Your menu

So whatever it takes
To get me where
You want me to be
This is my prayer

But, you know, Lord
I can't do this alone
Please hover over me closely
All the way home

February 5, 2004

FICKLE EYES

Lord, let me hear
Your voice today
Let me be quiet
Before You, I pray

For this is what
You want of me
My ears to hear
My eyes to see

For You came
To set me free
To give me life
Abundantly

You bid me to come
To stay by Your side
That's where You want
Me to abide

For in Your presence
That's when I know
There's no place else
I'd rather go

The love, the joy
The peace I feel
Nothing compares
Nothing's more real

I am complete
I am fulfilled
Everything is perfect
My soul is thrilled

The whole world dims
In the light of You
You change my perspective
You change my view

I vow I'll never
Leave Your side
I vow it's always
Here I will abide

But then I turn
Ever so slightly
It seems You're gone
I cry out to Thee

O God, where are You
Where did You go
Please don't leave me
I need You so

There's now a void
Where You once were
How did this happen
How did it occur

I struggle to find
My way back to You
I feel so empty
So alone and so blue

But You never left me
I finally realize
Twas not You who moved
But twas my eyes

They turned to focus
Another way
First for a moment
Then for a day

How fickle I am
I say I'll stay
But before I know it
I've gone away

Then once again
To You I cry out
I need You, Lord
I plead and I shout

And there You are
For You never left me
You're right here when I turn
My eyes back to Thee

February 13, 2004

MY DREAM

All my life I've been searching
For that one who would make my dreams come true
There has been a void inside of me
For I didn't know that one was You

I know You came to purchase and save me
To give me life and life more abundantly
Whatever I needed You said You would provide
You bid me to come, never again to run and hide

You gave me a dream, I now realize
It's been buried deep inside of me
For You told me many years ago
My ministry was to set Your people free

I didn't understand then, I barely do now
To what destination I am moving toward
I can't comprehend, the depth is too much
There's absolutely nothing Your love can't afford

I've had You, but I've still wanted more
I've yearned for something to make me complete
Surely this life has something to offer
More than just sorrow, heartache and defeat

This world is all I know, all I can see
Surely there's something here that can fulfill
I've searched and searched, I've waited and listened
Continually disappointed, dejected, unreal

When will I learn, when will I comprehend
What I'm searching for can't be contained in my hand
It is not something I can touch or feel
It is not made of flesh, stone, brick or land

If I could contain it in my hand, it would not last
I would have it for a moment, then it would disappear
Or it would tarnish, rust, rot or mildew
Or simply vanish like mist in the air

But still I keep searching, trying to find
That special something to make my dream come true
When will I realize, there's nothing in this world
That will satisfy or even begin to compare to You

When I let go of everything that's in this world
And concentrate wholly on You and who You are
That is when I'll be complete and whole
And I'll no longer need to search both near and far

Please come in and take up residence in me
So that my searching days will be over
You will be the only one I'll ever need
My food, my strength, my joy, my friend, my lover

For that is when my dreams will all come true
I'll have perfect love, which casts out all fear
I will do all things through Christ who strengthens me
And peace that passeth all understanding will be here

You are that Pearl of Great Price
The only thing I should be searching for
The only thing that can truly satisfy
My hope, my love, my sustenance, and so much more

So it is You, You are my dream
Why did I overlook, why did I not see
There's only one dream worth dreaming
That with You, in all Your glory, I might be

February 16, 2004

MESSAGE TO MY FRIENDS

Each friend is like a treasure
I find and hold so dear
Never to be forgotten
Whether far apart or near

Each one of you has touched me
In a very special way
More than you'll ever know
More than words can say

An emotional time this has been
In my life, you see
Some of you understand
You've walked the path ahead of me

Some of you don't have a clue
The things that I've walked through
There's no way you could comprehend
How much on the Lord I must depend

I didn't have a life before
I merely marked off days
I did what was expected
Conformed to others' ways

But, yet, I know
There is a strength in me
Put there by my Lord
So I will overcome, you see

My love for my Lord
Is the best thing I have to share

As I reach out to those around me
And let them know I care

I care if they are hurting
I care if they are sad
I want to make a difference
To make a sad heart glad

But sometimes in the process
Of searching out my way
I fumble and I stumble
And then I run away

If none of you have every done this
If you have it so all together
Then you are so truly blessed
To live in such sunny weather

Previously my emotions
Were always kept in check
No one was allowed to see
Emotions in me they didn't expect

So now, who am I?
Is there meaning to my life
Can I help to bring peace
Tear down contention and strife

For those things have been such a part
Of my life throughout the years
O God, I want to set others free
To love them and wipe away their tears

But only You, Lord, can do that
So a vessel I'm willing to be
Show me what to do and what to say
Through me, set Your people free

So back to you, my friends
At times I may seem strange
Because I've given my Lord the liberty
To remake, reform and rearrange

So during this time of struggling
Please make allowances for me
When you see me acting strangely
Just say a prayer for me to Thee

Apparently there's much work to be done
Inside of me, you see
So my life will have meaning
So I'll be all He meant for me to be

For this is my goal
This is my destiny
To be His, and His alone
And to help set His people free

February 23, 2004

MY PRAYER

Lord, where there is hatred
Let me show love
Love that comes from You
Pure and Holy from above

And where there is strife
May I always bring peace
Peace that passeth all understanding
That puts one's heart at ease

Where there is anger
Let me speak in a calm voice
To show the other person
They always have a choice

The choice is theirs to make
There is a better way
Before we give in to anger
We should always stop and pray

Pray that we will not sin
And let our anger come forth
But turn our minds toward good things
That have so much more worth

When I see someone hurting
Let me share their pain
Let me show how much You love them
That just for them, You came

When I know someone is lonely
Sense their dejection and despair
May I reach out in compassion
And let them know I care

In some whom I encounter
I will sense anxiety and fear
May I always have the right words
To show them You are near

You are always there just waiting
For us to turn to You
To show us that You love us
And tell us what to do

For those who are in bondage
Let me help to set them free
May the chains that so enslave them
Be broken for eternity

In my own strength, I cannot do this
On my own, there is no way
That I could change a single thing
Or make a difference in any day

But Your name, to me You have given
I have Your authority
To go forth to all the nations
To set the captives free

To preach the Gospel
To heal the brokenhearted
This anointing You have given
To me You have imparted

May I always use it wisely
May I correctly discern
Just what You would have me do
And never move or speak out of turn

May I never add to someone's sorrow
Never make a heartache worse
May I always be a blessing
And never, ever be a curse

O Lord, this is my prayer
This is my eternal plea
I want to be a vessel
To set Your people free

February 24, 2004

THE CHRIST

What can I possibly say
What can I do
When I think of the incomprehensible
Things they did to You

Twas not my hands that beat You
Twas not my mouth that mocked
But when I saw the way they treated You
I was stunned, horrified and shocked

There wasn't anything they could have done
To You that could be any worse
Than the things that You were subjected to
For me, You became a curse

You came in human form
You walked on earth as man
That's the way the Father intended
It was all in His plan

Nothing was a surprise
Nothing was left undone
You suffered the ultimate sacrifice
As on the cross You hung

We make it seem so glamorous
As we stand and sing our songs
That we have victory in Jesus
He took care of all our wrongs

Is that all we care about
That for us He paid the price
Now we can have life abundantly
All cozy, comfortable and nice

I feel so ashamed
I don't want to look in the mirror
For there I'll see the guilty one
I should have took all that furor

They beat Him to a pulp
Unrecognizable He was
Battered, whipped and pulverized
And they did it–just because

Just because they feared Him
They didn't understand
To them He was a threat
A different kind of man

Father, forgive them, He said
They know not what they do
After suffering such hideous agony
His thoughts were still on me and you

He would not give up
It had to be completed
Twas not for Himself He did it
But that we would not be defeated

He took our place
Upon that tree
Beaten and tortured
At Calvary

And what do we do
We usually complain
When life doesn't treat us
With prosperity and gain

We object to giving up
A meal to fast and pray

69

It's just not convenient
We'll do it another day

Procrastination and good intentions
Usually fill our days
We should be so thankful
Jesus had better ways

We need to bow before Him
Say, here I am, dear Lord
Do with me as You will
Let it be done, according to Your Word

Our lives no longer are our own
He purchased us with great price
How dare we demand our own way
After His ultimate sacrifice

February 25, 2004

MY LOVE FOR THEE

How do I love Thee?
Let me count the ways
I love You in the night time
And in the warm sun rays

I love You in the winter
In the summer and the fall
And when it is springtime
I love You best of all

I love You for who You are
And for Your great salvation
For Your loving care & concern
And especially for sanctification

Your loving kindness and mercy
Are definitely beyond compare
I could search o'er all the world
And find nothing like it anywhere

At times when I am so weary
You give me strength to carry on
And when life is dark and dreary
You put into my spirit a song

Even when I think
You are no where to be found
You are right here beside me
You said You'd always be around

I have no need to fret
I have no need to fear
For You have given me the promise
That You will always be near

There will never be one second
That Your presence I'll be without
I'll have You with me forever and ever
Of that I have no doubt

You order my footsteps
You map the road ahead of me
Your love is so perfect
There's no other place I'd rather be

Than right here by Your side
On the road that You have planned
I do not have to be anxious
For my hand is in Your hand

Your hand will never take me
To a place I should not go
I can truly put my trust in You
You'll never let me down, I know

So why would I not follow
A love that is so grand
There's no reason I can think of
Not to obey Your every command

When to do so fills me
With contentment and peace
Your way never brings confusion
But always brings pure release

Release from worldly cares
To a place of true rest
So when it comes to those I love
I'll always love You the best

April 2, 2004

WHO AM I?

Who am I
I am a child of God
Born of grace, mercy and love
Of Him who was sent from above

I was grafted into
His family tree
Evermore to be with Him
Throughout eternity

I am the righteousness of Christ
I've been redeemed and set free
And because of all He has done
I gladly give my life to Thee

Filled with His Spirit
In His presence I abide
Why, oh why, would I ever
Want to run away and hide

Those were days of yesteryear
Those days are gone and old
Today is a day of longing
His lovely face to behold

Oh, to look into those eyes
Such love I will find there
No other can hold a candle
No other can compare

I am His child
He has a plan for me
I want to fulfill that plan
I want to fulfill my destiny

I have the mind of Christ
I can tackle any task
If ever I lack wisdom
I only have to ask

For if He has called me to it
I'll have just what I need
To carry out His orders
When His every word I heed

I am peace and joy
I am love and mercy
Because I am His ambassador
He lives His life through me

Yes, I am redeemed
And, oh, what a price
Twas so very costly
What He did sacrifice

And He continues to give
So I'll have no lack
He's ever so faithful
And He takes nothing back

Now whenever I begin
To say who I am
I find myself telling
Of Him and His plan

Of myself, I am nothing
And I have nothing to give
Tis Jesus who is everything
It's His life I now live

April 3, 2004

ANOTHER DAY

Another day is before me
Will I grumble and complain
Or look on the brighter side
And faithfully praise Your name

Will I dread the things
I have to do today
Or will I remain in peace
And watch the things I say

For both life and death
Are in the power of my tongue
I can set myself up for failure
Or by my words the day can be won

There are so many good things
To be accomplished in this life
Every day should be peaceful
Void of contention and strife

May I look around me
And see someone in need
May I reach out to help
As Your prompting I heed

For You will always show me
The things I need to do
If I will watch and listen
And yield myself to You

It is not always easy
My flesh gets in the way
Sometimes I want to ignore
The things I hear You say

75

Obedience is better than sacrifice
It says so in Your Word
It's best to quickly move forward
When Your voice I know I've heard

You will not ask of me
A thing I cannot fulfill
And when I heed Your voice
I'll always be in Your will

I have no reason to worry
I have no need to fret
For You are always with me, and
You've never failed me yet

So I pray I will always
Keep my eyes on Thee
And listen to You carefully
Lord, this is my plea

For I want to be a vessel
One that's tried and true
One that You can trust
One that walks with You

I will take each day
One step at a time
As I keep in step with You
Never ahead or behind

For by Your side
Is where I'm called to be
Ever to do Your bidding
As through Your eyes I see

April 15, 2004

PEACE

My God loves me

I am the apple of His eye

He has great plans for me, plans to
prosper me and give me a great future

There is no one who loves me
more than my God

He sent His only Son to die for me

He goes to great lengths to take care of
me; I am important to Him

He cares about the little things in my life
just as much as the big things

He is always there; He will
never leave me

He causes my enemies to be at peace
with me

He gives me pure, sweet rest, and I
give Him my life

June 2, 2004

STAND WITH "I AM"

Know ye
That I AM God
And I'll rule one day
With an iron rod

Those who don't know Me
Shall melt away
But those who do
Forever will stay

In My presence
They will be
With Me forever
Throughout eternity

With Me they will
Rule and reign
Nothing will ever
Be the same

But until then
You must stand
With faith in Me
Your hand in My hand

I will lead you
I will guide you
Forever, I will be
Close beside you

Let go of those things
That weigh you down
Don't dwell on them
Or keep them around

Shake them off
Lighten your load
I will help you
To stay on My road

I will keep you
You will abide in Me
So stay close
And you will see

Miracles
As never before
Not once or twice
But many, many more

June 24, 2004

THE GLORIOUS BRIDE

Father, we think it's too difficult
There's too much to be done
There's no way we can do it all
So that souls will be won

It makes us so weary
Oh how bogged down we do feel
Is this something we can do?
Is it really real?

And then we look around us
So many faults we do see
A Bride without spot or wrinkle
We think we'll never be

It appears to be impossible
As through our own eyes we look
But what does our Lord say?
What does it say in His book?

That He will present to Himself
Without spot or wrinkle, His Bride
The Church in all her glory
She'll never want to run and hide!

For she will know
In whom she believes
She'll give no place or thought
To the one who deceives

For she abides in her Lord
His Word to perform
She's been washed in His Word
And to Him she does conform

The Bride of Christ
So beautiful is she
Oh, how her light will shine
O'er all the land and sea

What His Word says
Will surely come to pass
We must not doubt
But let our lips confess

That He is God
What He says, He will do
We can trust Him in everything
Knowing He'll see us through

June 25, 2004

WEDDED BLISS

They stand before the altar
Vow to stay together for life
Then they exchange rings
And become man and wife

It is so romantic
Special songs are sung
Then they leave together
Their married life has begun

The honeymoon is awesome
They have stars in their eyes
As they gaze at one another
It's true love, they realize

But somewhere down the road
Reality sets in
He's not all she thought he was
Contention and strife begin

To him, she seemed so perfect
On a pedestal so tall
Then he got a closer look
She's not so perfect after all

Now what happens
Where do they go from here
Can they make this work
year, after year, after year

He doesn't treat her right
It just isn't fair
Maybe she made a mistake
In this decision, she did err

Lord, what happened he says
Did I really hear from You
This woman You gave me
She just doesn't have a clue!

She's driving me nuts
As she constantly nags
I have to have some peace
I'll just go pack my bags

Let's face it
We made a mistake
What we thought was love
Has turned into hate

But God says "no"!
I joined you together
To stay with one another
Through both good and bad weather

Wife respect your husband
Don't treat him like a jerk
Husband love your wife
As Christ loves His church

Love her, protect her
A covering you are to be
Treat her with loving kindness
She'll change, you'll see

It won't happen instantly
There will be rough roads some days
But if you each seek Christ
You'll slowly change your ways

Serve one another
Don't demand your own way
Treasure the gift God gave you
You'll be truly thankful one day

It's not easy, it takes work
I know, you didn't count on this
But if you seek Christ and His ways obey
You can have wedded bliss!

July 14, 2004

LIVING WATER

Some days I see so clearly
There are no shadows at all
While other days are fuzzy
Shadows on every wall

On the clear days, I can see
Far, far into eternity
Every little thing makes sense
Tis the way it was meant to be

But on the days of shadows
On me, the walls close in
I can't do the things I want to do
I don't even know where to begin

Why does my life fluctuate so
Some days there is little peace
Regardless of what I do or say
I cannot find that sacred release

I search within myself
I want to understand
I need to find some sense
In everything at hand

Life is such a struggle
It's more than I can bear
I'll just drift off into oblivion
Pretend I don't have a care

Wouldn't that be easier
No burdens to bear
Just drift off into nothingness
No heartaches to share

But if life is to have meaning
I must know where to turn
I must know my Creator
For His touch I must yearn

Without Him I can do nothing
Life will never make sense
One long, continuous struggle
A life lived in pretense

But with Him, all things are possible
No more sorry or woe
He shines a light on all darkness
Leads me in the path that I should go

So turn, I tell myself
Turn and seek His face
You do not have to struggle
You've been saved by grace

This grace will lift you up
Out of the miry clay
This grace will keep your feet
On the King's highway

So struggle no more
Myself, I do tell
But immerse yourself
Into His deep well

That well of living water
Let it wash over me
Then, again, I see clearly
Far, far into eternity

July 22, 2004

SEARCH FOR MORE

Of what should I write
O Great and Holy One
Of things of You
New and under the sun

Can we know more
Of things this day
Of what You do
And what You say

You hold the seasons
You number the days
We have limited knowledge
Of Your fearful ways

Child, I've separated you
For a reason
Accept My decision
For your every season

Be content
In where you are
Don't strive to search
For that distant star

I've provided you with
Your every need
And My every word
I ask you to heed

Lord, am I not to search
For more of You
Way far beyond
The sky so blue

There must be more
Than what I know
My heart does yearn
I need You so

I will give you more
In My own time
Be patient, child
And just be Mine

Your days are numbered
As in My plan
But there are some things
I do not share with man

You would not comprehend
You would not understand
If I were to reveal all things
To happen in the land

I will share with you
In My own time
The things you need to know
Because you are Mine

Until then
Keep your faith strong
I'm not to be trifled with
So separate right from wrong

Feed My sheep
Each one is your brother
And just follow Me
Don't listen to another

August 14, 2004

DARE TO BELIEVE

Is it any different now
Than it was then
There are those who truly believe
And those who live in sin

There are those who ridicule
All the things of God
They have no time for Him
As on their own they trod

There are those who don't understand
The things set forth in His Word
Just figments of someone's imagination
Mere stories someone has heard

There are those who become angry
When someone talks of the Lord
They do not want to hear such talk
Or any mention of His Word

There are those who are afraid
That He might make them change
They like their life the way it is
And want nothing rearranged

Someone tried to change them once
They've heard it all before
It's just a bunch of nonsense
Of which they want no more

There are those who think they're right
They have it all figured out
They've changed the very context
Of what it's all about

There are those who've been derailed
By one of those mentioned above
They can no longer believe
In God and all His love

But it cannot be changed
It cannot be watered down
It must be accepted as is
Yes, God did come to town!

He created the world
Formed man and wife
He breathed into them
And gave them life

They disobeyed
So paradise they lost
God would get them back
But at a very high cost

He did come
And walk on earth
Then He died and rose again
All so we could have rebirth

Yes, to be born again
To know His glory
That's what it's all about
Jesus and His story

But it's not just a story
It's real and, oh, so grand
Won't you take Him at His Word
And put your hand in His hand?

August 19, 2004

LOVE THAT CHERISHES

Make her feel special
That woman in your life
Let her know you love her
Your girlfriend or wife

Don't be afraid
Your feelings to show
For exactly how you feel
She really wants to know

If you'll look into her eyes
And tell her that you care
That the rest of your life
With her you'd like to share

You'll make her so happy
She'll love you in return
The love will never die
But through eternity will burn

She needs to be cherished
She needs to feel your love
A love that has been ordained
Straight from God above

Don't take her for granted
Sure she'll always be around
Let her know a treasure
In her you have found

If she's your girlfriend
Then make her your wife
And pledge to always love her
For the rest of your life

A real man will do this
He's not afraid to love
For this love was given
By his Father from above

Any man can tear down
The woman in his life
But a truly Godly man
Will bring healing to his wife

Contention and strife
Were never meant to be
A part of the relationship
Of the union of he and she

So if you are struggling
Things are not the way they were
Ask God to rekindle
What you used to feel for her

God can bring it back again
The things you once did feel
He'll bring an even deeper love
And it will be ever so real

Only God can show you how
To be a man and yet be tender
How to be the head
And still be her defender

Protect her, cherish her
Give honor where it's due
And you will be rewarded
For she'll always treasure you

September 6, 2004

GOING HIS WAY

The path I'm on
Is not one I would choose
It took a turn I do not like
If not my choice, then whose

This is not the way
I prefer to spend my days
Did I make a wrong turn
Into a world filled with haze

Doctors and tests
Procedures and rest
Confinement and boredom
Where did this come from

The steps of a righteous man
Are ordered by the Lord
Tis not my opinion
It says so in His Word

What are You trying to tell me
What do You want to say
Did I go off on a tangent
Did I go off on my own way

Maybe I did
But not necessarily so
It may just be an adjustment
In the way He would have me go

Sometimes my priorities
Are different from His
I want to pass the test
If this is a quiz

It's time to get quiet
Quiet before Him
To ignore and continue on
For *me* would be sin

I have given Him my life
To do with as He will
For me to retract anything
Could certainly make me ill

My life is not my own
I've been bought with a price
Lord, let me never forget
Your costly sacrifice

It's time to pull away
And spend more time with You
The hours I spend with man
Should be kept to just a few

There are many good things
That I can find to do
But they are not right for me
If not ordered by You

So quiet before You
Again I will get
The cares of this world
Shall not make me fret

My life again
To You I give
Please show me each day
The way I must live

September 19, 2004

COME, MY BELOVED

Come away, My beloved
Spend time alone with Me
Come ever so close
So close that you can see

My every detail
What I AM all about
Nothing will be a mystery
In you there'll be no doubt

I want to dine with you
And tender moments share
You'll learn just who you are
You'll know how much I care

To Me you are so precious
I created you, you know
I grieve when you are hurting
I long to make you whole

If you will come to Me
And let Me wash you clean
You'll be the greatest miracle
This world has ever seen

Transformation, without a doubt
Is the best thing that I do
If you will yield yourself to Me
I'll make something beautiful of you

So again I say, please come
Spend some time with Me
And peace I'll give to you
For all the world to see

September 20, 2004

I'M YOURS

Lord, I come
And bow down to You
To You, I give myself
For whatever You want to do

I am Thine
Your will to be done
Because You have called
Tis why I have come

I'm nothing without You
So lost on my own
If I had not found You
Through life I would roam

Seeking and searching
Trying to find
Something to give me
Just a little peace of mind

But coldness and darkness
Is all I would find
For unless I have You
I have life of no kind

Nothing that's real
That will truly satisfy
I have to have You
And I know the reason why

You are my Creator
Only You can make me whole
So here I am, dear Lord
I give to You my soul

September 21, 2004

LIFE

I searched and I searched
Trying to find
Something to give me
A little peace of mind

I did a little of this
A little of that
Like trying to pull life
Out of a hat

I'd leap without looking
Hoping this time
This thing called happiness
Would finally be mine

I had a yearning
Down deep inside
I searched for fulfillment
Both far and wide

But regardless of what
I did or I found
Contentment and peace
Were never around

Then finally I cried
Is there any happiness for me
Or in this dark dungeon
Will I always be

Then I saw the light
On me it did shine
Twas Christ Jesus
And He said He was mine

I stopped and I turned
To Him I did yield
And then I saw the mystery
That to me had been concealed

Now I have life
And life abundantly
I found it in Christ
The One who died for me

If you don't know Him
He's waiting for you
To invite Him in
Then you'll have life, too

September 21, 2004

ARISE AND BE HEALED

Oh healing virtue
Where are you
Are you out there somewhere
Beyond the blue

With sickness and sorrow
We do strive
Fighting for each breath
Just to stay alive

The struggle is endless
No peace in sight
Oh, that we could
Just give up the fight

Everything seems futile
All hope is gone
But it's always the darkest
Just before dawn

The light will come
Of that be sure
A bright and shining light
Ever so pure

It shines out
From His Word
The most beautiful Word
Ever to be heard

Take His Word
Consume it as your own
And throughout your body
Let it roam

Let His Word get
To every part
To your hands and feet
From your head to your heart

His Word is vital
Without it we die
We shrivel into nothing
Become brittle and dry

We must soak ourselves
In this Word
The Words of Jesus
Must be heard

Out of our mouth
Into our ear
Daily we must eat
Daily we must hear

And then we will live
So come awake, oh my soul
Arise and be healed
Completely whole

October 21, 2004

OUR LIFELINE

How sad You must be
When You look down on earth
You paid the price for blessings
We still cling to the curse

You came to show us how to live
All we know is how to die
You came to bring us true life
We cling to unbelief and strife

We want to succeed
So we tear down one another
But we can never succeed
At the expense of our brother

It's a corrupt world
Without a doubt
But You came, dear Lord
To show us the way out

It's not what's around us
That gives us a hope
It's what's inside us
A lifeline, a rope

Something to hold onto
A love that will not fail
That love, when we call on it
Will always prevail

You came, You lived, You died
On the third day arose again
You paved the way for all mankind
You said we could call You friend

Why do we carry on
As if You never came
You came to change us
But we remain the same

You knock at our hearts
You want to come in
To bring us Your love
To overcome sin

We open the door
We invite You in
It sounds oh so good
And we do want to win

But we don't embrace
You completely, Lord
We try to carry on
Without Your Word

Your Word will change us
A new creature we'll be
When we truly walk with You
A difference we will see

Your Word, Your love, Your life
That's all we need to know
You have everything we need
To live, to love, to grow

We must let go of the world
And cling only to You
You are that rope, that lifeline
Only You give us hope so true

October 26, 2004

LOVE THAT PREVAILS

Wife respect your husband
Do not tear him down
Let him know you admire him
And love to have him around

Be considerate of his needs
Don't scoff at his advice
And to ignore his counsel
Really isn't very nice

Though he is the head of your home
You are to walk side by side
Helping one another along the way
Be a true partner, and never chide

Be careful of your appearance
Keep yourself neat and clean
Don't neglect your time with the Lord
For His love through you should be seen

The Lord must come first in your life
Without Him you shall surely fail
You must seek Him every day
And let His love through you prevail

As you spend time with Him
And meditate on His Word
He will change you on the inside
Exceedingly more than what you've heard

Submit yourself unto the Lord
Give Him free rein in your life
To make you what He meant you to be
An obedient daughter, a loving wife

When you are full of His love
It will overflow on those around
But it must begin with Him
No greater love can be found

It is easy to be a loving wife
To gladly do your part
When the love of God
Is shed abroad in your heart

So if you want your marriage
To be everything it can be
You must start with the Lord
He is the only way, you see

He came to bring us life
And life more abundantly
So marriage should be a uniting
Not of two, but three

Without Him you will be miserable
Without Him you will fail
So let Him be Lord of your life
And watch His love through you prevail

November 4, 2004

YOUR WAY, NOT MINE

Sometimes it seems
There's no reason to go on
I feel so alone
My reason for living is gone

The days run together
My life seems adrift
There's no reason to continue
Nothing to give my heart a lift

Why am I still here
I wonder so oft
You still have a purpose
Comes His voice so soft

I have to struggle
Sometimes to hear His voice
It's one I need to hear
O Lord, do I have a choice

I just keep going
Day after day
Hoping that soon
I'll find my way

Lord, I know You're there
And I know that You do care
So empty I should not feel
Because I know Your love is real

Yet there are times like these
When I sit here all alone
I can't help but wonder
Why can't I, too, just go home

And then I'm reminded
There's a reason I am here
I must put my trust in You
And never, ever fear

And You I must diligently seek
To become all You want me to be
I must not give up so soon
Even though Your face I long to see

There is more for me to do
You have not called me yet
Please show me how to carry on
What to remember, what to forget

I want to accomplish
All You have for me to do
So I can be complete and ready
When I hear that call from You

May Your perfect will
Be accomplished in me
May I be all
That You want me to be

I want to run the race
And reach the finish line
With all the assurance
I did it Your way, not mine

So help me each day
To look to You
To rejoice and be thankful
For Your love so true

November 8, 2004

THANK YOU, GOD

You came to us
From Heaven above
You came to show us
How to really love

You left the glory
And splendor behind
You came to be just another
One of mankind

You were God
But You became man
It wasn't an accident
It was part of Your plan

God as a baby
Grew here on earth
More than a magnificent story
Was that virgin birth

As a boy, then a man
You lived, and You hurt
As You walked the dusty roads
On Your feet there was dirt

When did you realize
Who You really were
How long did it take
For that truth to occur

Or did You always know
That in the Father You did abide
A carpenter by trade
Yet God inside

How did You feel
Did you seem all alone
Was it foreign to You on earth
Did You long to go home

I can't imagine
How here on earth You did trod
But then I can't imagine
What it would be like to be God

There are those who think
That God does not exist
And in their vain philosophies
They continue to persist

For them, I feel so sad
They think it's just a story
They do not believe in God
Or Heaven and all it's glory

But though my eye has not seen
And my ear has not heard
I believe in my heart
In God and His Word

Nothing can separate me
From God or His Son
Or the comfort of the Holy Spirit
That Holy Three-in-One

I don't understand
Why You chose Calvary
But Lord, I want to thank You
For doing this just for me

December 9, 2004

A NEW YEAR, A NEW LIFE

Good morning, dear Lord
It's now 2005
I pray this year
In You I'll come alive

I know the plans I have
For you, My child
Plans for a future
So warm and mild

I'll never do you harm
So listen to My voice
Your future lies in Me
I am your best choice

Don't heed your own voice
Don't go your own way
For I have plans for you
If by My side you'll stay

I tried to direct you
Many years ago
You chose to ignore me
You chose a life of woe

Even then
I stayed by your side
I tried to draw you to Me
So in Me you would abide

It has been a struggle
Over the years
You've had some successes
You've also had tears

You've gone through some things
You had to go through
Trials and testings
Have now made you true

True to Me
My daughter, at last
You can look to the future
No longer the past

The past is over
A new life I bring
The tears are gone
Now you will sing

A new song to Me
You will sing each day
As you come to Me
To show you the way

Your way will be solid
Stable and true
For My life will shine
From Me to you

It is My pleasure
Dear child of Mine
To fill your life
With things divine

Thank You, dear Lord
To You I'll be true
I'll listen to Your voice
I'll wait on You

January 1, 2005

HIS PLAN, HIS PATH

I cannot go
By my own plan
I cannot walk
The steps of man

My steps would falter
And turn the wrong way
For my feet are
But feet of clay

But His feet are
Of iron and brass
They will not wither
As dew on the grass

They are true
The steps of God
And they have gone
Where no man can trod

He has walked the path
Ahead of me
He has plotted out
My destiny

For I would turn
When He would go straight
And I would run
When He would say wait

He has taught me how
To wait on Him
Not to plow ahead
On my every whim

111

For my every whim
Would lead to pain
And usually to loss
Rather than gain

Though things at the time
To me would seem right
They would turn my day
Into the blackest night

It didn't have
To be this way
He has always wanted
To lead me each day

So no longer do
I journey on my own
But I wait on Him
To show me the way home

Home is where He is
And where I want to be
Now He lights my path
So every step I'll see

He does this for me
Because of my choice
To follow Him
To listen to His voice

You, too
Can follow His path
He will lead you
You just have to ask

January 6, 2005

REPENT AND SUBMIT

Sin is sin, and there's
Nothing glamorous about it
It hurts, it shames, it destroys
Over and over I'll shout it

I shout to the people
Beware!
Admonish everyone
Take care!

Take care to do
The things that are right
Beware of things
You seek out at night

The Lord is watching
He sees everything
Your sins will find you out
And sorrow they will bring

You think you're justified
To feel the way you do
You think you have a right
To do the things you do

I'm here to say
You don't
And if you do
God won't

God won't send you blessings
When you disobey
You'll bring on yourself the curses
Around it, there's no way

So who are you going to serve
You must decide today
Are you going to serve the Lord
Or will you go your own way

You think you're okay
All on your own
You can take care of yourself
As o'er the world you roam

But I'm here to say
You're on a dead end street
If you continue on that road
Trouble you will meet

The lusts of the flesh
The pride of life
Quarreling and jealousy
Contention and strife

Are all a part
Of Satan's snare
He'll reel you in
Without a care

If you are wise
You will repent
Twas for forgiveness
That Jesus was sent

He paid the price
For you to win
But you must submit
And let Him in

January 6, 2005

JESUS, HE'S MINE

Jesus, I pray
That I will come
To really know You
As God's son

That You will be
Someone to me
Who I will treasure
Throughout eternity

For even now
Here on earth
You're the one who gave
To me new birth

Born again
Oh what glory
I love You, Jesus
I love Your story

You are my High Tower
The one I run to
When'er I have trouble
You see me through

When I am calm
Together we sit
You're always right there
And we talk a bit

When I am weary
You understand
For though You're God
You lived as man

You know my heart
My every weakness
Yet you don't condemn
Or of me think less

Your love to me
It overflows
My love for You
Just grows and grows

Never before
Have I known such love
But then I wasn't looking
To things above

Now I am searching
And I have found
That Pearl of Great Price
Who'll always be around

You'll always be here
Just a prayer away
And whenever I ask
You come to stay

Close beside me
What comfort You give
Without You I wouldn't
Know how to live

You are so beautiful
Lovely, divine
Please, dear Jesus
Always be mine

January 7, 2005

CHANGED, BUT STILL ME

I bring my life
To You
To do with as
You want to do

That does not mean
I have to be
Stripped of everything
That makes me, me

But I give myself
To You to mold
Into a better shape
Your love to hold

I yield myself
To my Creator
To smooth out the flaws
To make me better

So that the things
That I see
I now see through
The eyes of Thee

My goals and ambitions
You change
My concept of life
You rearrange

I give you liberty
To make me over
Not just to cloak me
With a different cover

You change me from
The inside out
It seems you change
What I am all about

But the same spirit
You formed in me
From the very beginning
To be like Thee

Is still there
It now shines through
It has become stronger
And more like You

All the qualities You
Put inside of me
Are more useful now
You've set me free

Free to be
Who You designed
But more like You
Than like mankind

More peace, more joy
More contentment, it's true
My thoughts have changed
They stay on You

I still could do
What I want to do
But it's so much better
When I yield to You

January 8, 2005

THE ROAD TO JESUS

I cried out to You
In 1983
Lord, please make me what
You meant for me to be

And over the years
You've done Your part
To cleanse and mold
And change my heart

Sometimes I yielded
Sometimes I would balk
At times You carried me
When I couldn't walk

It wasn't easy
The road to You
There were many trials
I had to go through

But You never promised
All sunshine and gain
You said in each life
There would be some rain

There were many times
Along the way
I couldn't tell the difference
Between night and day

I wondered if
You were still there
I couldn't feel You
And I didn't have a prayer

Yet, there were times
I could see so clear
And at those times
I knew You were near

Yes, You have answered
That cry of mine
And made me into something
Much more divine

Still, I'm not so dense
That I believe
There is no longer
Any sin in me

So search me, O Lord
Please, and see
If there be any wicked
Way in me

As I yield again
And before You bow
For I've come too far
To lose out now

January 9, 2005

DO WE REALLY LOVE HIM?

I love You, Lord
We often say
I need You, Lord
We often pray

But then we trot off
On our own
On a journey
All alone

We forget our love
And need for Him
And before we know it
We're deep in sin

It may not seem
Like sin to you
There's just no time
His will to do

Your schedule is
Too full, at best
There's never even
Time for rest

I'd gladly serve Him
You do say
If He'd just help me
Find a way

I've said these things
Before myself
And the things of God
I've put on the shelf

For there were too
Many things to do
Something had to give
And, guess who?

Oh, yes, twas God
No time for Him
Oh, but be careful
For that is sin

The sin of omission
We will find
Will be the downfall
Of many mankind

For if you love Him
His commandments you will keep
If you love Him
More of Him you will seek

He's standing there waiting
Knocking on your door
You've kept it closed in the past
But here's a change once more

January 9, 2005

LOVE

What is it really
This thing called love
An action, an emotion
Or something from above

We talk about it
And about it we sing
We know of the feelings
That it can bring

But do we know
What true love is
Is it only those feelings
Of hers or his

Or is it something
Much deeper than this
More than attraction
Or wedded bliss

Oh, yes
It is much more
It causes us to live
And it's something to die for

The author of love
Is God, the Father
Who gave us Jesus
As friend and brother

He became our Savior
On Calvary
When He willingly died
For you and me

Redeeming love
Oh, how divine
And it encompasses
All mankind

Oh, how He loves
You and me
If only you'd open
Your eyes and see

Please don't miss
This great love
That was sent to us
From God above

Nothing on this earth
Could ever compare
With His great love
And it's everywhere

If you'll but open
Your eyes, you'll see
A bird, a flower
A mountain or a tree

They are His signature
His Word is true
Everything He created
For me and you

And that is love
My friend, you see
Unfailing love
For you and me

January 10, 2005

INDEX

Contact author Carol Breeden
or order more copies of this book at

TATE PUBLISHING, LLC

127 East Trade Center Terrace
Mustang, Oklahoma 73064

(888) 361 - 9473

Tate Publishing, LLC

www.tatepublishing.com